contents

NZ, Canada, US and UK readers
Please note that Australian cup and spoon measurements are metric. A conversion chart appears on page 62.

ALL ABOUT

Old-fashioned desserts are the much-loved family recipes that have been enjoyed for generations. Treats such as creamy cheesecake, quivering baked custard, crusty apple pie or baked stuffed apples are the stuff memories are made of. In baking of any description, there are some rules of thumb that, if followed, will lead to perfect results, every time. Because baking recipes are almost scientifically devised, they rely on exact measures. When measuring your flour, sugar and other ingredients, ensure you use metric cup and spoon measures, filled to level with the top. A good set of scales is an invaluable tool in the kitchen to get weights correct. Specific pans have been chosen for each dessert for particular reasons so be sure to use the right kind and grease or line exactly as directed in the recipe.

BAKING

And, if you're wondering what to do with leftover egg yolks or whites, they can be frozen for up to three months. Freeze, individually, in an ice-cube tray then transfer to a freezer container. Egg yolks need to be stabilised before freezing by adding a pinch of salt or 1½ teaspoons of sugar to every four yolks (depending on whether they will be used for sweet or savoury dishes after thawing). Thaw overnight in the refrigerator before using.

banana caramel tart

395g can sweetened condensed milk
75g butter, chopped coarsely
½ cup (110g) firmly packed brown sugar
2 tablespoons golden syrup
2 large bananas (460g), sliced thinly
300ml thickened cream, whipped

pastry

1½ cups (225g) plain flour
1 tablespoon icing sugar
140g cold butter, chopped coarsely
1 egg yolk
2 tablespoons cold water

1 Make pastry.
2 Grease 24cm-round loose-based fluted flan tin. Roll dough between sheets of baking paper until large enough to line tin. Ease dough into tin; press into base and side. Trim edge; prick base all over with fork. Cover; refrigerate 30 minutes.
3 Preheat oven to 200°C/180°C fan-forced.
4 Place tin on oven tray; cover dough with baking paper, fill with dried beans or rice. Bake 10 minutes; remove paper and beans carefully from pie shell. Bake a further 10 minutes; cool.
5 Meanwhile, combine condensed milk, butter, sugar and syrup in medium saucepan; cook over medium heat, stirring, about 10 minutes or until mixture is caramel coloured. Stand 5 minutes; pour into pie shell, cool.
6 Top caramel with banana; top with whipped cream.

pastry Process flour, icing sugar and butter until crumbly; add egg yolk and water. Process until ingredients come together. Knead dough on floured surface until smooth. Wrap in plastic; refrigerate 30 minutes.

preparation time 45 minutes (plus refrigeration time)
cooking time 35 minutes
serves 8

apple pie

1½ cups (225g) plain flour
¾ cup (110g) self-raising flour
⅓ cup (50g) cornflour
½ cup (60g) custard powder
185g cold butter, chopped coarsely
1 tablespoon white sugar
1 egg, separated
⅓ cup (80ml) iced water, approximately
2 tablespoons apricot jam
2 teaspoons white sugar, extra

apple filling

7 large green-skinned apples (1.5kg)
½ cup (125ml) water
¼ cup (55g) white sugar
½ teaspoon ground cinnamon
1 teaspoon finely grated lemon rind

1 Make apple filling.

2 Sift flours and custard powder into large bowl; rub in butter then stir in sugar. Make well in centre, add egg yolk and enough of the water to mix to a firm dough; knead lightly. Cover; refrigerate 1 hour.

3 Preheat oven to 200°C/180°C fan-forced.

4 Roll out just over half the pastry, on floured surface, until just large enough to line a 23cm pie plate. Lift pastry into pie plate; press into side, trim edge. Spread base of pastry with apricot jam, top with filling.

5 Roll out remaining pastry until large enough to cover pie. Brush edges of pie with a little lightly beaten egg white; cover with pastry. Press edges together firmly, trim and decorate. Brush pastry with egg white; sprinkle with extra sugar. Cut a few slits into pastry to allow steam to escape.

6 Bake about 25 minutes or until golden brown.

apple filling Peel, quarter and core apples; cut each quarter in half lengthways. Combine apples in large saucepan with the water, sugar, cinnamon and rind. Bring to the boil; simmer, covered, about 5 minutes or until apples are almost tender. Remove from heat; drain, cool to room temperature.

preparation time 45 minutes
(plus cooling and refrigeration time)
cooking time 35 minutes
serves 8

pecan pie

2 cups (280g) roasted pecans
6 egg yolks
½ cup (175g) golden syrup
½ cup (110g) firmly packed brown sugar
90g butter, melted
¼ cup (60ml) thickened cream

pastry

1¼ cups (185g) plain flour
⅓ cup (55g) icing sugar
125g cold butter, chopped coarsely
1 egg yolk
1 teaspoon lemon juice

1 Grease 24cm-round loose-based flan tin.

2 Make pastry.

3 Place nuts in pastry case. Combine egg yolks, syrup, sugar, butter and cream in small bowl; whisk until smooth. Pour mixture over nuts; bake, about 30 minutes or until set. Cool. Serve with cream, if desired.

pastry Blend or process flour, icing sugar and butter until combined. Add egg yolk and juice; process until ingredients just come together. Knead dough on floured surface until smooth. Cover; refrigerate 30 minutes. Roll dough between sheets of baking paper until large enough to line prepared tin. Ease dough into tin, press into side; trim edge. Cover; refrigerate 30 minutes. Preheat oven to 180°C/160°C fan-forced. Place tin on oven tray. Line pastry case with baking paper, fill with dried beans or rice. Bake, 15 minutes. Remove paper and beans; bake, about 5 minutes or until browned lightly.

preparation time 25 minutes (plus refrigeration time)
cooking time 50 minutes
serves 8
tip This recipe can be made a day ahead.

impossible pie

This dessert is called "impossible" because, while a runny mixture is poured into the cake pan, it is a three-layered "pie" that emerges from the oven. The bottom layer is pastry-like because the flour and butter sink to the bottom; the centre layer is like a custard filling; and the top is slightly browned and crusty because the coconut, the lightest ingredient, floats to the top during baking.

½ cup (75g) plain flour
1 cup (220g) caster sugar
¾ cup (60g) desiccated coconut
4 eggs
1 teaspoon vanilla extract
125g butter, melted
½ cup (40g) flaked almonds
2 cups (500ml) milk

1 Preheat oven to 180°C/160°C fan-forced. Grease deep 24cm pie dish.
2 Combine sifted flour, sugar, coconut, eggs, extract, butter and half the nuts in large bowl; gradually add milk, stirring, until combined. Pour into dish; bake 35 minutes.
3 Remove pie from oven. Sprinkle remaining nuts over pie; bake 10 minutes. Serve pie with cream, if desired.

preparation time 10 minutes
cooking time 45 minutes
serves 8
tip Store impossible pie, covered, in the refrigerator, for up to two days.

lemon tart

1¼ cups (185g) plain flour
⅓ cup (55g) icing sugar
¼ cup (30g) almond meal
125g cold butter, chopped coarsely
1 egg yolk

lemon filling

1 tablespoon finely grated lemon rind
½ cup (125ml) lemon juice
5 eggs
¾ cup (165g) caster sugar
1 cup (250ml) thickened cream

1 Blend or process flour, icing sugar, almond meal and butter until combined. Add egg yolk; process until ingredients just come together. Knead dough on floured surface until smooth. Wrap in plastic wrap, refrigerate 30 minutes.
2 Roll pastry between sheets of baking paper until large enough to line 24cm-round loose-based flan tin. Lift pastry into tin; press into side, trim edge. Cover; refrigerate 30 minutes.
3 Meanwhile, preheat oven to 200°C/180°C fan-forced.
4 Place flan tin on oven tray. Line pastry case with baking paper, fill with dried beans or rice. Bake, 15 minutes. Remove paper and beans; bake about 10 minutes or until browned lightly.
5 Meanwhile, make lemon filling.
6 Reduce oven temperature to 180°C/160°C fan-forced.
7 Pour lemon filling into pastry case; bake about 30 minutes or until filling has set slightly. Cool.
8 Refrigerate until cold. Serve dusted with sifted icing sugar, if desired.

lemon filling Whisk ingredients in medium bowl; stand 5 minutes.

preparation time 30 minutes (plus refrigeration time)
cooking time 55 minutes
serves 8
tips You need about three lemons for this tart. Best made a day ahead; keep, covered, in the refrigerator.

lemon meringue pie

½ cup (75g) cornflour
1 cup (220g) caster sugar
½ cup (125ml) lemon juice
1¼ cups (310ml) water
2 teaspoons finely grated lemon rind
60g unsalted butter, chopped coarsely
3 eggs, separated
½ cup (110g) caster sugar, extra

pastry

1½ cups (225g) plain flour
1 tablespoon icing sugar
140g cold butter, chopped coarsely
1 egg yolk
2 tablespoons cold water

preparation time 30 minutes (plus refrigeration time)
cooking time 35 minutes
serves 10
tip Lemon meringue is best made and eaten the same day.

1 Make pastry.

2 Grease 24cm-round loose-based fluted flan tin. Roll pastry between sheets of baking paper until large enough to line tin. Ease pastry into tin, press into base and side; trim edge. Cover; refrigerate 30 minutes.

3 Preheat oven to 240°C/220°C fan-forced.

4 Place tin on oven tray. Line pastry case with baking paper; fill with dried beans or rice. Bake 15 minutes; remove paper and beans carefully from pie shell. Bake about 10 minutes; cool pie shell, turn off oven.

5 Meanwhile, combine cornflour and sugar in medium saucepan; gradually stir in juice and the water until smooth. Cook, stirring, over high heat, until mixture boils and thickens. Reduce heat; simmer, stirring, 1 minute. Remove from heat; stir in rind, butter and egg yolks. Cool 10 minutes.

6 Spread filling into pie shell. Cover; refrigerate 2 hours.

7 Preheat oven to 240°C/220°C fan-forced.

8 Beat egg whites in small bowl with electric mixer until soft peaks form; gradually add extra sugar, beating until sugar dissolves.

9 Roughen surface of filling with fork before spreading with meringue mixture. Bake about 2 minutes or until browned lightly.

pastry Process flour, icing sugar and butter until crumbly. Add egg yolk and the water; process until ingredients come together. Knead dough on floured surface until smooth. Cover; refrigerate 30 minutes.

baked cheesecake

250g plain sweet biscuits
125g butter, melted
½ teaspoon mixed spice
cream cheese filling
4 eggs
¾ cup (165g) caster sugar
500g cream cheese
1 tablespoon finely grated lemon rind

1 Process biscuits until fine. Add butter, process until combined. Press mixture over base and side of 20cm springform tin. Place tin on oven tray; refrigerate 30 minutes.

2 Preheat oven to 160°C/140°C fan-forced.

3 Make cream cheese filling.

4 Pour filling into tin; bake about 50 minutes. Cool in oven with door ajar. Refrigerate 3 hours or overnight.

5 Serve cheesecake sprinkled with mixed spice.

cream cheese filling Beat eggs and sugar in small bowl with electric mixer until thick and creamy. Beat cream cheese and rind in medium bowl with electric mixer until smooth. Add egg mixture to cheese mixture; beat until combined.

preparation time 20 minutes (plus refrigeration time)
cooking time 50 minutes
serves 10

lemon cheesecake

250g packet plain sweet biscuits
125g butter, melted
250g packet cream cheese, softened
395g can sweetened condensed milk
2 teaspoons finely grated lemon rind
⅓ cup (80ml) lemon juice
1 teaspoon gelatine
1 tablespoon water

1 Blend or process biscuits until mixture resembles fine breadcrumbs. Add butter; process until combined. Press biscuit mixture evenly over base and side of 20cm springform tin, place on oven tray; refrigerate about 30 minutes or until firm.
2 Meanwhile, beat cream cheese in small bowl with electric mixer until smooth. Beat in condensed milk, rind and juice; beat until smooth.
3 Sprinkle gelatine over the water in small heatproof jug; stand jug in small saucepan of simmering water. Stir until gelatine dissolves; cool 5 minutes.
4 Stir gelatine mixture into lemon mixture. Pour mixture into crumb crust; cover cheesecake, refrigerate about 3 hours or until set.

preparation time 30 minutes (plus refrigeration time)
serves 8
tip This recipe can be made a day ahead; keep, covered, in the refrigerator.

chocolate mousse

200g dark eating chocolate
300ml thickened cream
3 eggs, separated
2 tablespoons caster sugar

1 Break off and reserve a long piece of the chocolate, weighing about 25g, for making decorative chocolate shavings.
2 Chop remaining chocolate coarsely then combine it with half the cream in large heatproof bowl. Place bowl over saucepan of simmering water (see tip); stir until chocolate has melted. Cool chocolate mixture 5 minutes then quickly stir in egg yolks, one at a time.
3 Beat egg whites in small bowl on highest speed with electric mixer until soft peaks form; add sugar, beat until dissolved. Gently fold whites, in two batches, into chocolate mixture; pour mixture into four ⅔-cup (160ml) serving glasses. Refrigerate 3 hours or overnight.
4 Whip remaining cream until soft peaks form. Make chocolate shavings by running a vegetable peeler along one edge of the reserved piece of chocolate. Dollop cream and sprinkle chocolate over each mousse.

preparation time 15 minutes (plus refrigeration time)
cooking time 5 minutes
serves 4
tips When melting chocolate, take care it doesn't come into contact with the water. If it does, it will "seize", that is, become lumpy and lose its sheen. If this occurs, you'll have to start over with a new piece of chocolate.
When the yolks are stirred into the melted chocolate mixture, work quickly and stir rapidly to avoid the yolks "scrambling" in the still warm mixture.

chocolate self-saucing pudding

1 cup (150g) self-raising flour
½ teaspoon bicarbonate of soda
½ cup (50g) cocoa powder
1¼ cups (275g) firmly packed brown sugar
80g butter, melted
½ cup (120g) sour cream
1 egg, beaten lightly
2 cups (500ml) boiling water

1 Preheat oven to 180°C/160°C fan-forced. Grease deep 1.5-litre (6-cup) ovenproof dish.
2 Sift flour, soda, half the cocoa and ½ cup of the sugar into medium bowl; stir in combined butter, sour cream and egg.
3 Spread mixture into prepared dish. Sift remaining cocoa and remaining sugar evenly over mixture; gently pour over the boiling water.
4 Bake, about 40 minutes. Stand 5 minutes before serving with vanilla ice-cream, if desired.

preparation time 10 minutes
cooking time 40 minutes
serves 6

lemon delicious pudding

125g butter, melted
2 teaspoons finely grated lemon rind
1½ cups (330g) caster sugar
3 eggs, separated
½ cup (75g) self-raising flour
⅓ cup (80ml) lemon juice
1⅓ cups (330ml) milk

1 Preheat oven to 180°C/160°C fan-forced. Grease six 1-cup (250ml) ovenproof dishes.
2 Combine butter, rind, sugar and yolks in large bowl. Stir in sifted flour then juice. Gradually stir in milk; mixture should be smooth and runny.
3 Beat egg whites in small bowl with electric mixer until soft peaks form; fold into lemon mixture, in two batches.
4 Place ovenproof dishes in large baking dish; divide lemon mixture among dishes. Add enough boiling water to baking dish to come halfway up sides of ovenproof dishes. Bake, about 45 minutes.

preparation time 20 minutes
cooking time 45 minutes
serves 6

steamed pudding

60g butter
¼ cup (90g) golden syrup
½ teaspoon bicarbonate of soda
1 cup (150g) self-raising flour
2 teaspoons ground ginger
½ cup (125ml) milk
1 egg

golden syrup sauce

⅓ cup (115g) golden syrup
2 tablespoons water
30g butter

1 Grease 1.25-litre (5-cup) pudding steamer.
2 Combine butter and syrup in small saucepan; stir over low heat until smooth. Remove from heat, stir in soda; transfer mixture to medium bowl. Stir in sifted dry ingredients then combined milk and egg, in two batches.
3 Spread mixture into steamer. Cover with pleated baking paper and foil; secure with lid.
4 Place pudding steamer in large saucepan with enough boiling water to come halfway up side of steamer; cover pan with tight-fitting lid. Boil 1 hour, replenishing water as necessary to maintain level. Stand pudding 5 minutes before turning onto plate.
5 Meanwhile, make syrup.
6 Serve pudding topped with syrup and, if desired, cream.
golden syrup sauce Stir ingredients in small saucepan over heat until smooth; bring to the boil. Reduce heat; simmer, uncovered, 2 minutes.

preparation time 15 minutes
cooking time 1 hour
serves 6

sticky date pudding with butterscotch sauce

1¼ cups (200g) seeded dried dates
1¼ cups (310ml) boiling water
1 teaspoon bicarbonate of soda
50g butter, chopped coarsely
½ cup (100g) firmly packed brown sugar
2 eggs, beaten lightly
1 cup (150g) self-raising flour

butterscotch sauce

¾ cup (150g) firmly packed brown sugar
300ml cream
80g butter

1 Preheat oven to 180°C/160°C fan-forced. Grease deep 20cm-round cake pan; line base with baking paper.

2 Combine dates and the water in medium heatproof bowl. Stir in soda; stand 5 minutes.

3 Blend or process date mixture with butter and sugar until pureed. Add eggs and flour; blend or process until just combined. Pour mixture into prepared pan.

4 Bake, in oven, about 1 hour (cover with foil if pudding starts to overbrown). Stand 10 minutes; turn onto serving plate.

5 Meanwhile, make butterscotch sauce. Serve pudding warm with butterscotch sauce.

butterscotch sauce Combine ingredients in medium saucepan; stir over low heat until sauce is smooth and slightly thickened.

preparation time 10 minutes
cooking time 1 hour
serves 6
tips Both the pudding and sauce can be made a day ahead; store, covered separately, in the refrigerator.
You can freeze the pudding for up to three months. Defrost and warm in the microwave oven while making the butterscotch sauce.

bread and butter pudding

6 (270g) thin slices white bread
40g butter, softened
4 eggs
⅓ cup (75g) caster sugar
3½ cups (875ml) milk
1 teaspoon vanilla extract
½ cup (80g) sultanas
ground nutmeg

1 Preheat oven to 160°C/140°C fan-forced.

2 Trim crusts from bread; butter each slice then cut each slice into four triangles. Arrange two rows of triangles, butter-side up, overlapping slightly, along base of shallow 2-litre (8 cup) ovenproof dish. Centre another row of triangles over first two rows, with triangles facing in opposite direction to triangles in first layer.

3 Whisk eggs, sugar, milk and extract in bowl. Pour half the custard mixture over bread; stand 10 minutes.

4 Whisk remaining custard mixture again; add sultanas then pour into dish. Sprinkle with nutmeg. Stand dish in larger baking dish; add enough boiling water to come halfway up side of dish.

5 Bake about 50 minutes or until custard is set. Serve this pudding hot or cold, with stewed fruit and ice-cream, if you like.

preparation time 20 minutes
cooking time 50 minutes
serves 4
tips This recipe can be made a day ahead; store, covered, in the refrigerator.
Substitute any dried fruit of your choice for the sultanas in this recipe.
Use ground cinnamon instead of the ground nutmeg, if you prefer.

summer pudding

Summer pudding is commonly made using stale bread; we've developed our own version with a twist, using homemade sponge cake.

3 eggs
½ cup (110g) caster sugar
1 tablespoon cornflour
¾ cup (110g) self-raising flour
1 teaspoon butter
¼ cup (60ml) boiling water
⅓ cup (75g) caster sugar, extra
½ cup (125ml) water
2 cups (300g) frozen blackberries
3⅓ cups (500g) frozen mixed berries
¼ cup (80g) blackberry jam

1 Preheat oven to 180°C/160°C fan-forced. Grease 25cm x 30cm swiss roll pan; line base with baking paper, extending paper 5cm over long sides.

2 Beat eggs in small bowl with electric mixer until thick. Gradually add sugar, beating until sugar dissolves; transfer mixture to large bowl.

3 Fold triple-sifted flours into egg mixture. Pour combined butter and boiling water down side of bowl; fold into egg mixture. Spread mixture into pan; bake 15 minutes. Cool in cake pan.

4 Combine extra sugar and the water in medium saucepan; bring to the boil. Stir in berries; return to the boil. Simmer, uncovered, until berries soften. Strain over medium bowl; reserve syrup and berries separately.

5 Line 1.25-litre (5-cup) pudding basin with plastic wrap, extending wrap 10cm over side of basin. Cut circle slightly smaller than top edge of basin from cake; cut second circle exact size of base of basin from cake. Cut remaining cake into 10cm long strips.

6 Place small cake in base of basin and use cake strips to line side of basin. Pour ⅔ cup of the syrup into small jug; reserve. Fill basin with berries; cover with remaining syrup, top with large cake. Use overhanging plastic wrap to cover pudding, weight pudding with saucer; refrigerate 3 hours or overnight.

7 Stir jam and two tablespoons of the reserved syrup in small saucepan until heated through. Turn pudding onto serving plate; brush with remaining reserved syrup then jam mixture. Serve with whipped cream, if desired.

preparation time 30 minutes (plus refrigeration time)
cooking time 25 minutes
serves 6

profiteroles

75g butter
¾ cup (180ml) water
¾ cup (110g) plain flour
3 eggs

crème pâtissière

2¼ cups (560ml) milk
1 vanilla bean, split lengthways
6 egg yolks
⅔ cup (150g) caster sugar
½ cup (75g) plain flour

chocolate liqueur sauce

100g dark eating chocolate, chopped coarsely
30g butter
⅓ cup (80ml) cream
1 tablespoon orange-flavoured liqueur

preparation time 45 minutes (plus refrigeration and cooling time)
cooking time 35 minutes
makes 36
tips You can use Cointreau, Grand Marnier, Curaçao or any other orange-flavoured liqueur in this recipe.

1 Make crème pâtissière.

2 Preheat oven to 200°C/180°C fan-forced. Lightly grease two oven trays.

3 Combine butter with the water in medium saucepan; bring to the boil. Add flour; beat with wooden spoon over heat until mixture forms a smooth ball. Transfer mixture to small bowl; beat in eggs, one at a time, with electric mixer until mixture becomes glossy.

4 Drop teaspoons of dough 4cm apart on trays; bake in oven about 7 minutes or until pastries puff. Reduce oven temperature to 180°C/160°C fan-forced; bake 10 minutes or until browned lightly and crisp.

5 Cut a small slit in base of each profiterole; bake a further 5 minutes or until profiteroles dry out. Cool before filling with crème pâtissière.

6 Meanwhile, make chocolate liqueur sauce.

7 Spoon or pipe crème pâtissière through cuts into profiteroles. Serve profiteroles drizzled with chocolate liqueur sauce.

crème pâtissière Bring milk and vanilla bean to the boil in medium saucepan; remove from heat. Stand 10 minutes; discard bean. Beat yolks and sugar in bowl with electric mixer until thick; beat in sifted flour. With motor operating on low speed, gradually beat in hot milk mixture. Return mixture to saucepan; stir over heat until mixture boils and thickens. Simmer, stirring, 2 minutes. Remove from heat; transfer to medium bowl. Cover surface with plastic wrap to prevent skin forming; refrigerate until cold.

chocolate liqueur sauce Stir chocolate, butter and cream in small saucepan over low heat until smooth. Stir in liqueur.

baked custard

6 eggs
1 teaspoon vanilla extract
⅓ cup (75g) caster sugar
1 litre (4 cups) hot milk
¼ teaspoon ground nutmeg

1 Preheat oven to 160°C/140°C fan-forced. Grease shallow 1.5-litre (6-cup) ovenproof dish.
2 Whisk eggs, extract and sugar in large bowl; gradually whisk in hot milk. Pour custard mixture into dish; sprinkle with nutmeg.
3 Place dish in larger baking dish; add enough boiling water to come halfway up sides of dish. Bake about 45 minutes. Remove custard from large dish; stand 5 minutes before serving.

variations

citrus Stir ½ teaspoon each of finely grated orange, lime and lemon rind into hot milk mixture; omit nutmeg.
chocolate Whisk ⅓ cup cocoa powder and ⅓ cup dark Choc Bits with eggs, extract and sugar; omit nutmeg.
coconut and cardamom Omit hot milk; bring 2⅓ cups milk, 400ml can coconut milk, 3 bruised cardamom pods and 5cm strip lime rind to the boil. Remove from heat, stand 10 minutes. Strain; discard solids. Whisk milk mixture into egg mixture.

preparation time 5 minutes
cooking time 45 minutes
serves 6

baked rice custard

4 eggs
⅓ cup (75g) caster sugar
½ teaspoon vanilla extract
2 cups (500ml) milk
300ml cream
⅓ cup (50g) raisins
1½ cups cold cooked white medium-grain rice
1 teaspoon ground cinnamon

1 Preheat oven to 180°C/160°C fan-forced. Grease 1.5-litre (6-cup) baking dish.
2 Whisk eggs, sugar and extract in medium bowl until combined. Whisk in milk and cream; stir in raisins and rice.
3 Pour mixture into dish. Place dish in large baking dish; pour enough boiling water into baking dish to come halfway up sides of dish. Bake 30 minutes, whisking lightly with fork under skin occasionally. Sprinkle with cinnamon; bake 20 minutes. Serve warm or cold.

preparation time 10 minutes
cooking time 50 minutes
serves 6
tip Store, covered, in the refrigerator, for up to two days.

creamed rice

1 litre (4 cups) milk
⅓ cup (75g) caster sugar
1 teaspoon vanilla extract
½ cup (100g) uncooked white medium-grain rice

1 Combine milk, sugar and extract in large saucepan; bring to the boil. Gradually add rice to boiling milk. Reduce heat; simmer, covered, stirring occasionally, about 50 minutes or until rice is tender and milk is almost absorbed.
2 Serve warm or cold, with fresh berries, if desired.

preparation time 5 minutes
cooking time 50 minutes
serves 4
tip Store, covered, in the refrigerator, for up to two days.

apple and rhubarb crumble

You'll need to buy a bunch of rhubarb weighing about a kilo in order to get the 600g of chopped stems needed here.

4 medium green-skinned apples (600g)
20g butter
¼ cup (50g) firmly packed brown sugar
5½ cups (600g) coarsely chopped rhubarb
2 tablespoons orange juice
2 cups (60g) corn flakes, crushed slightly
½ cup (35g) shredded coconut
⅓ cup (75g) firmly packed brown sugar, extra
2 tablespoons plain flour
70g butter, chopped coarsely

1 Preheat oven to 180°C/160°C fan-forced.
2 Peel and core apples; cut into thick wedges. Melt butter in large saucepan; cook apple and sugar, stirring, until sugar dissolves and apple just starts to caramelise. Add rhubarb and juice; cook, stirring, until rhubarb is tender. Transfer mixture to 1.5-litre (6-cup) ovenproof dish.
3 Combine corn flakes, coconut, extra sugar and flour in large bowl. Using fingers, rub chopped butter into crumble mixture.
4 Spoon crumble mixture evenly over top of apple rhubarb mixture; bake, in oven, about 15 minutes or until crumble is golden brown. Serve with vanilla ice-cream, if desired.

preparation time 15 minutes
cooking time 30 minutes
serves 4
tips The leaves of rhubarb are high in oxalic acid, which can be toxic when eaten in a large quantity, so these, and the trimmed top and bottom of the stem, should be discarded. Shredded coconut is the dried flesh, sliced into very thin strips. It's best to use this for a crumble rather than the desiccated coconut, which is too fine for the crumble topping.

baked apples

4 large green-skinned apples (800g)
50g butter, melted
⅓ cup (75g) firmly packed brown sugar
½ cup (80g) sultanas
1 teaspoon ground cinnamon

1 Preheat oven to 160°C/140°C fan-forced.
2 Core unpeeled apples about three-quarters of the way down from stem end, making hole 4cm in diameter. Use a small sharp knife to score around centre of each apple.
3 Combine remaining ingredients in small bowl. Pack sultana mixture firmly into apples; stand apples upright in small baking dish. Bake, about 45 minutes.

variations

muesli filling Replace sultana mixture with ⅔ cup natural muesli, 1 cup thawed, well-drained frozen blueberries, 40g melted butter and 2 tablespoons brown sugar.

berry filling Replace sultana mixture with 1½ cups thawed well-drained frozen mixed berries. Bruise 4 cardamom pods; place one cardamom pod in each apple with mixed berries.

preparation time 15 minutes
cooking time 45 minutes
serves 4

poached pears with chocolate cream

4 medium pears (920g), peeled, halved, cored
1 litre (4 cups) water
1 cinnamon stick
1 vanilla bean, halved lengthways
½ cup (110g) white sugar
200g dark eating chocolate, chopped coarsely
½ cup (125ml) cream

1 Combine pears, the water, cinnamon, vanilla bean and sugar in medium saucepan; stir over medium heat until sugar is dissolved. Bring to the boil; simmer, covered, about 8 minutes or until pears are just tender, drain.

2 Meanwhile, combine chocolate and cream in small saucepan; stir over low heat about 5 minutes or until smooth.

3 Pour chocolate cream over pears to serve; add a scoop of vanilla ice-cream, if you like.

preparation time 15 minutes
cooking time 15 minutes
serves 4
tips The pears can be poached a day ahead. Canned pears could be substituted for fresh pears to save time.
The chocolate cream is best made close to serving.

classic trifle

85g packet raspberry jelly crystals
250g store-bought sponge cake
2 tablespoons raspberry jam
¼ cup (60ml) sweet sherry
¼ cup (30g) custard powder
¼ cup (55g) caster sugar
1½ cups (375ml) milk
825g can sliced peaches, drained
1 teaspoon vanilla extract
1½ cups (375ml) thickened cream
2 tablespoons flaked almonds, roasted

1 Make jelly according to directions on packet; pour into a shallow container (such as a cake pan). Cover and refrigerate 20 minutes or until jelly is almost set.

2 Meanwhile, split cake in half, spread bottom half of the cake with jam; replace top. Cut into 3cm pieces.

3 Arrange cake pieces in 3.5-litre (14-cup) serving dish; sprinkle with sherry.

4 Combine custard powder, sugar and 1 tablespoon of the milk in small saucepan; stir in remaining milk. Stir over heat until mixture boils and thickens. Cover surface with damp baking paper or cling wrap to prevent a skin forming; cool.

5 Pour almost-set jelly over cake, cover; refrigerate 15 minutes or until jelly is set. Arrange the peach slices over the jelly.

6 Stir extract and ½ cup of the cream into custard; pour over peaches.

7 Whip remaining cream, spread over custard; sprinkle with flaked almonds. Refrigerate several hours or overnight.

preparation time 25 minutes (plus refrigeration time)
cooking time 10 minutes
serves 8

crème caramel

¾ cup (165g) caster sugar
½ cup (125ml) water
300ml cream
1¾ cups (430ml) milk
6 eggs
1 teaspoon vanilla extract
⅓ cup (75g) caster sugar, extra

preparation time 20 minutes (plus refrigeration time)
cooking time 40 minutes
serves 6

1 Preheat oven to 160°C/140°C fan-forced.

2 Combine sugar and the water in medium frying pan; stir over heat, without boiling, until sugar dissolves. Bring to the boil; boil, uncovered, without stirring, until mixture is a deep caramel colour. Remove from heat; allow bubbles to subside. Pour toffee into deep 20cm-round cake pan.

3 Bring cream and milk to the boil in medium saucepan. Whisk eggs, extract and extra sugar in large bowl. Whisking constantly, pour hot milk mixture into egg mixture. Strain mixture into cake pan.

4 Place pan in medium baking dish; add enough boiling water to come half way up side of pan. Bake, in oven, about 40 minutes or until firm. Remove custard from baking dish, cover; refrigerate overnight.

5 Gently ease crème caramel from side of pan; invert onto deep-sided serving plate.

variations

vanilla bean Add 1 split vanilla bean to cream and milk mixture before bringing to the boil; strain. Remove bean; add milk to egg mixture.

orange Stir 2 teaspoons finely grated orange rind into custard mixture before baking.

hazelnut Add 1 cup coarsely chopped roasted hazelnuts to cream and milk mixture; bring to the boil. Cover; stand 20 minutes then strain through muslin-lined sieve. Discard nuts. Bring cream and milk mixture back to the boil before whisking into egg mixture.

cinnamon Add 1 cinnamon stick to cream and milk mixture before bringing to the boil; strain, remove cinnamon stick before adding to egg mixture.

pavlova

4 egg whites
1 cup (220g) caster sugar
½ teaspoon vanilla extract
¾ teaspoon white vinegar
300ml thickened cream, whipped
250g strawberries

1 Preheat oven to 120°C/100°C fan-forced. Line oven tray with foil. Grease foil, dust with cornflour; shake away excess. Mark an 18cm-circle on foil.
2 Beat egg whites in small bowl with electric mixer until soft peaks form; add half the sugar, beat until dissolved. Gradually add remaining sugar, beating after each addition. When sugar is dissolved, add extract and vinegar; beat until combined.
3 Spread meringue into circle on foil, building up sides to approximately 8cm high.
4 Carefully smooth sides and top of pavlova then, with spatula blade, mark decorative grooves round side of pavlova; smooth top again.
5 Bake about 1½ hours; pavlova should be firm to touch. Turn off oven, cool pavlova in oven with door ajar.
6 When pavlova is cold, cut around top edge; the crisp meringue top will fall slightly on top of the marshmallow. Serve pavlova topped with cream and strawberries; lightly dust with sifted icing sugar, if desired.

preparation time 25 minutes (plus cooling time)
cooking time 1 hour 30 minutes
serves 8
tip Pavlova can be made a day ahead; keep in an airtight container. Top with cream and strawberries just before serving.

custard tart

1¼ cups plain flour
¼ cup self-raising flour
¼ cup caster sugar
90g cold butter,
  chopped coarsely
1 egg
2 teaspoons water,
  approximately
ground nutmeg

custard filling

3 eggs
1 teaspoon vanilla extract
2 tablespoons caster sugar
2 cups milk

1 Sift flours and sugar into bowl, rub in butter. Add egg and enough water to make ingredients cling together. Press dough into a ball; knead on floured surface until smooth. Cover; refrigerate 30 minutes.

2 Preheat oven to 200°C/180°C fan-forced.

3 Roll dough on floured surface until large enough to line 23cm pie plate. Lift pastry into pie plate, gently ease into side of plate; trim edge.

4 Place pie plate on oven tray; line pastry with baking paper, fill with dried beans or rice. Bake 10 minutes. Remove paper and beans; bake further 10 minutes or until pastry is browned lightly, cool.

5 Meanwhile, make custard. Pour custard into pastry case; bake 15 minutes. Sprinkle custard evenly with nutmeg; bake further 15 minutes or until custard is just set, cool. Refrigerate until cold.

custard filling Whisk eggs, extract and sugar in bowl until combined. Heat milk until hot; quickly whisk into egg mixture.

preparation time 15 minutes (plus refrigeration and cooling time)
cooking time 1 hour
serves 6
tip Recipe can be made a day ahead and stored, covered, in the refrigerator.

apple strudel

1kg apples
¼ cup (60ml) water
1 teaspoon grated lemon rind
1 clove
½ teaspoon ground cinnamon
½ teaspoon ground nutmeg
2 tablespoons almond meal
¾ cup (75g) walnuts, chopped coarsely
¾ cup (120g) sultanas
5 sheets fillo pastry
60g butter, melted
2 tablespoons almond meal, extra
icing sugar, for dusting

1 Peel, core, quarter and thinly slice apples; combine in large saucepan with water, rind and clove. Cover; cook about 10 minutes or until apples are tender. Discard clove; cool apple mixture.
2 Preheat oven to 180°C/160°C fan-forced.
3 Combine cold apple mixture in bowl with spices, almond meal, nuts and sultanas.
4 Layer pastry sheets together, brushing each with butter and sprinkling with extra almond meal. Spread filling over pastry, leaving 2cm boarder down long sides and 5cm at each end. Fold in ends then roll up like a swiss roll.
5 Place strudel on greased oven tray, brush with butter. Bake about 40 minutes or until browned lightly.
6 Dust strudel with sifted icing sugar before serving. Serve warm or cold with custard or cream, if desired.

preparation time 15 minutes (plus cooling time)
cooking time 50 minutes
serves 6
tip Recipe can be made a day ahead; keep, covered, in the refrigerator.

chocolate sundaes

2 litres vanilla ice-cream
100g marshmallows
12 ice-cream wafers
½ cup (70g) crushed nuts

hot chocolate sauce

200g dark eating chocolate, chopped coarsely
½ cup (125ml) thickened cream

1 Make hot chocolate sauce.
2 Place a little of the hot chocolate sauce in the base of six ¾-cup (180ml) serving glasses; top with ice-cream, marshmallows, wafer biscuits and more chocolate sauce. Sprinkle with nuts, serve immediately.

hot chocolate sauce Combine chocolate and cream in small saucepan; stir over low heat until chocolate is melted and sauce is smooth, do not overheat.

preparation time 5 minutes
cooking time 5 minutes
serves 6

glossary

almonds flat, pointy-ended nuts with pitted brown shell enclosing a creamy white kernel that is covered by a brown skin.
flaked paper-thin slices.
meal also known as ground almonds; nuts are powdered to a coarse flour-like texture.

bicarbonate of soda also known as baking or carb soda.

blind baking is a cooking term used to describe baking a pie shell or pastry case before the filling is added. If a filling does not need to be baked, or is very wet, it may be necessary to "blind bake" the unfilled shell. To blind bake, ease the pastry into a pan or dish and place on an oven tray. Line the pastry with baking paper then fill with dried beans, uncooked rice or "baking beans" (also called pie weights). Bake according to the recipe's directions then cool before adding the filling. Uncooked rice or dried beans used to weigh down the pastry are not suitable for eating. Use them every time you bake blind; cool, then store in an airtight jar.

biscuits also called cookies.

butter use salted or unsalted (sweet) butter; 125g is equal to one stick (4 ounces) of butter.

chocolate
choc Bits also known as chocolate chips or morsels; available in milk, white and dark chocolate. Made of cocoa liquor, cocoa butter, sugar and an emulsifier; they hold their shape in baking and are ideal for decorating.
choc Melts discs of dark milk or white chocolate ideal for melting and moulding.
dark eating also known as semi-sweet or luxury chocolate; made of cocoa liquor, cocoa butter and a little added sugar.

cinnamon the dried inner bark of the shoots of the cinnamon tree; available both in sticks (quills) or ground, as powder.

cocoa powder also known as cocoa; dried, unsweetened, roasted then ground cocoa beans.

coconut
desiccated unsweetened, concentrated, dried, finely shredded coconut.
shredded thin strips of dried coconut.

corn flakes commercially manufactured cereal made of dehydrated then baked crisp flakes of corn. Also available is a prepared finely ground mixture used for coating or crumbing food before frying or baking, sold as "crushed corn flakes" in 300g packages in most supermarkets.

cornflour also known as cornstarch; used as a thickening agent in cooking.

cream we used fresh cream, also known as pure cream and pouring cream, unless otherwise stated.
cheese commonly known as Philadelphia or Philly; a soft cows-milk cheese.
sour a thick commercially-cultured soured cream.
thickened a whipping cream containing a thickener.

custard powder instant mixture used to make pouring custard; similar to North American instant pudding mixes.

dates fruit of the date palm tree, eaten fresh or dried. About 4cm to 6cm in length, oval and plump, thin-skinned, with a honey flavour and sticky texture.

fillo pastry (also filo or phyllo) tissue-thin pastry sheets purchased chilled or frozen from supermarkets.

flour
plain an all-purpose flour, made from wheat.
self-raising plain flour sifted with baking powder in the proportion of 1 cup flour to 2 teaspoons baking powder.

gelatine we use powdered gelatine. Also available in sheet form known as leaf gelatine. Two teaspoons of powdered gelatine (7g or one sachet) is roughly equivalent to four gelatine leaves.

ginger, ground also known as powdered ginger; used as a flavouring in cakes, pies and puddings. It cannot be substituted for fresh ginger.

golden syrup a by-product of refined sugarcane; pure maple syrup or honey can be substituted.

hazelnuts also known as filberts; plump, grape-size, rich, sweet nut having a brown inedible skin that is removed by rubbing heated nuts together vigorously in a tea-towel.

ice-cream wafers a crisp, very thin, flat biscuit most often eaten with ice-cream.

jam also known as preserve or conserve; a thickened mixture of fruit and sugar.

jelly crystals a powdered mixture of gelatine, sweetener, and artificial fruit flavouring used to make a moulded, translucent, quivering dessert. Also known as jello.

mixed spice a blend of ground spices usually consisting of cinnamon, allspice and nutmeg.

nutmeg the dried nut of an evergreen tree native to Indonesia; it is available in ground form or you can grate your own with a fine grater.

pecans native to the United States and now grown locally; a golden-brown, buttery, rich tasting nut.

pine nuts also known as pignoli; not in fact a nut but a small, cream-coloured kernel from pine cones.

pistachio pale green, delicately flavoured nut inside hard off-white shells. To peel, soak shelled nuts in boiling water for about 5 minutes; drain, then pat dry with absorbent paper. Rub skins with cloth to peel.

raisins dried sweet grapes.

rice

arborio small, round-grain rice well-suited to absorb a large amount of liquid, which gives rice dishes a rich, classic creaminess.

white medium-grain also known as calrose rice; extremely versatile rice that can be substituted for short- or long-grain rices if necessary.

savoiardi also known as savoy biscuits, lady's fingers or sponge fingers; they are Italian-style crisp fingers made from sponge-cake mixture.

sugar

brown a very soft, finely granulated sugar retaining molasses for its colour and flavour.

caster also known as finely granulated or superfine table sugar.

icing sugar also known as confectioners' sugar or powdered sugar; granulated sugar crushed together with a small amount of cornflour.

white coarse, granulated table sugar, also known as crystal sugar.

sultanas dried grapes, also known as golden raisins.

sweet sherry fortified wine consumed as an aperitif or used in cooking.

sweetened condensed milk a canned milk product consisting of milk with more than half the water content removed and sugar added to the remaining milk.

vanilla

bean dried, long, thin pod from a tropical golden orchid grown in central and South America and Tahiti; the tiny black seeds inside the bean impart a luscious vanilla flavour. Place a whole bean in a jar of sugar to make the vanilla sugar often called for in recipes; a bean can be used three or four times before losing its flavour.

extract obtained from vanilla beans infused in water; a non-alcoholic version of essence.

vinegar

white made from spirit of cane sugar.

brown malt made from fermented malt and beech shavings.

walnut the kernel of the walnut is ridged and oval and formed in two distinct halves. Can be substituted for pecans.

conversion chart

MEASURES

One Australian metric measuring cup holds approximately 250ml, one Australian metric tablespoon holds 20ml, one Australian metric teaspoon holds 5ml.

The difference between one country's measuring cups and another's is within a 2- or 3-teaspoon variance, and will not affect your cooking results. North America, New Zealand and the United Kingdom use a 15ml tablespoon. All cup and spoon measurements are level. The most accurate way of measuring dry ingredients is to weigh them. When measuring liquids, use a clear glass or plastic jug with metric markings.

We use large eggs with an average weight of 60g.

DRY MEASURES

METRIC	IMPERIAL
15g	½oz
30g	1oz
60g	2oz
90g	3oz
125g	4oz (¼lb)
155g	5oz
185g	6oz
220g	7oz
250g	8oz (½lb)
280g	9oz
315g	10oz
345g	11oz
375g	12oz (¾lb)
410g	13oz
440g	14oz
470g	15oz
500g	16oz (1lb)
750g	24oz (1½lb)
1kg	32oz (2lb)

LIQUID MEASURES

METRIC	IMPERIAL
30ml	1 fluid oz
60ml	2 fluid oz
100ml	3 fluid oz
125ml	4 fluid oz
150ml	5 fluid oz (¼ pint/1 gill)
190ml	6 fluid oz
250ml	8 fluid oz
300ml	10 fluid oz (½ pint)
500ml	16 fluid oz
600ml	20 fluid oz (1 pint)
1000ml (1 litre)	1¾ pints

LENGTH MEASURES

METRIC	IMPERIAL
3mm	⅛in
6mm	¼in
1cm	½in
2cm	¾in
2.5cm	1in
5cm	2in
6cm	2½in
8cm	3in
10cm	4in
13cm	5in
15cm	6in
18cm	7in
20cm	8in
23cm	9in
25cm	10in
28cm	11in
30cm	12in (1ft)

OVEN TEMPERATURES

These oven temperatures are only a guide for conventional ovens. For fan-forced ovens, check the manufacturer's manual.

	°C (CELSIUS)	°F (FAHRENHEIT)	GAS MARK
Very slow	120	250	½
Slow	150	275 – 300	1 – 2
Moderately slow	160	325	3
Moderate	180	350 – 375	4 – 5
Moderately hot	200	400	6
Hot	220	425 – 450	7 – 8
Very hot	240	475	9

index

Are you missing some of the world's favourite cookbooks?

The Australian Women's Weekly cookbooks are available from bookshops, cookshops, supermarkets and other stores all over the world. You can also buy direct from the publisher, using the order form below.

MINI SERIES £3.50 190x138MM 64 PAGES

TITLE	QTY	TITLE	QTY	TITLE	QTY
4 Fast Ingredients		Easy Pies & Pastries		Pickles and Chutneys	
15-minute Feasts		Finger Food		Pasta	
50 Fast Chicken Fillets		Fishcakes & Crispybakes		Potatoes	
50 Fast Desserts		Gluten-free Cooking		Quick Desserts	
After-work Stir-fries		Grills & Barbecues		Roast	
Barbecue Chicken		Healthy Everyday Food 4 Kids		Salads	
Bites		Ice-creams & Sorbets		Simple Slices	
Bowl Food		Indian Cooking		Simply Seafood	
Burgers, Rösti & Fritters		Italian Favourites		Skinny Food	
Cafe Cakes		Jams & Jellies		Soup Plus	
Cafe Food		Japanese Favourites		Spanish Favourites	
Casseroles		Kebabs & Skewers		Stir-fries	
Casseroles & Curries		Kids Party Food		Stir-fry Favourites	
Char-grills & Barbecues		Last-minute Meals		Summer Salads	
Cheesecakes, Pavlova & Trifles		Lebanese Cooking		Tagines & Couscous	
Chinese Favourites		Low-Fat Delicious		Tapas, Antipasto & Mezze	
Christmas Cakes & Puddings		Malaysian Favourites		Tarts	
Christmas Favourites		Mince		Tex-Mex	
Cocktails		Mince Favourites		Thai Favourites	
Crumbles & Bakes		Muffins		The Fast Egg	
Cupcakes & Cookies		Noodles		Vegetarian	
Curries		Noodles & Stir-fries		Vegie Main Meals	
Dips & Dippers		Old-Fashioned Desserts		Vietnamese Favourites	
Dried Fruit & Nuts		Outdoor Eating		Wok	
Drinks		Party Food		TOTAL COST £	

Photocopy and complete coupon below

ACP Magazines Ltd Privacy Notice
This book may contain offers, competitions or surveys that require you to provide information about yourself if you choose to enter or take part in any such Reader Offer.
If you provide information about yourself to ACP Magazines Ltd, the company will use this information to provide you with the products or services you have requested, and may supply your information to contractors that help ACP to do this. ACP will also use your information to inform you of other ACP publications, products, services and events. ACP will also give your information to organisations that are providing special prizes or offers, and that are clearly associated with the Reader Offer.
Unless you tell us not to, we may give your information to other organisations that use it to inform you about other products, services and events or who may give it to other organisations that may use it for this purpose. If you would like to gain access to the information ACP holds about you, please contact ACP's Privacy Officer at:
ACP Magazines Ltd, 54-58 Park Street, Sydney, NSW 2000, Australia

☐ Privacy Notice: Please do not provide information about me to any organisation not associated with this offer.

Name ____________________

Address ____________________

____________________ Postcode ____________

Country ____________ Phone (business hours) ____________

Email*(optional) ____________________

* *By including your email address, you consent to receipt of any email regarding this magazine, and other emails which inform you of ACP's other publications, products, services and events, and to promote third party goods and services you may be interested in.*

I enclose my cheque/money order for £ ________ or please charge £ ________

to my: ☐ Access ☐ Mastercard ☐ Visa ☐ Diners Club

Card number | | | | | | | | | | | | | | | | |

3 digit security code *(found on reverse of card)* ____________

Cardholder's signature ____________________ Expiry date ____ /____

To order: Mail or fax – photocopy or complete the order form above, and send your credit card details or cheque payable to: Australian Consolidated Press (UK), 10 Scirocco Close, Moulton Park Office Village, Northampton NN3 6AP, phone (+44) (01) 604 642200, fax (+44) (01) 604 642300, e-mail books@acpuk.com or order online at www.acpuk.com
Non-UK residents: We accept the credit cards listed on the coupon, or cheques, drafts or International Money Orders payable in sterling and drawn on a UK bank. Credit card charges are at the exchange rate current at the time of payment.
All pricing current at time of going to press and subject to change/availability.
Postage and packing UK: Add £1.00 per order plus 75p per book.
Postage and packing overseas: Add £2.00 per order plus £1.50 per book. **Offer ends 31.12.2008**